Traverse City

from Farmstead to Lakeshore

Traverse City
from Farmstead to Lakeshore

THOMAS KACHADURIAN

All inquiries should be addressed to:
Ann Arbor Media Group LLC.
2500 S. State Street
Ann Arbor, MI 48104

Printed and bound in Canada.

10   9   8   7   6   5   4   3   2   1

Library of Congress Cataloging-in-Publication data on file.

ISBN-13: 978-1-58726-302-6
ISBN-10: 1-58726-302-5

To contact the author visit www.kachadurian.com

Chateau Grand Traverse, View to West Grand Traverse Bay

Hometown

Traverse City is what you see in it—a place that depends on your perspective. It's well known as a vacation spot, either as a jumping off place or as a final destination. Air travelers flying to anywhere in the entire region have a TVC tag hanging from their bags. To Benzonians, Bellairians, and Bretherenites, Traverse City is the closest big city for a shopping trip. To one other group—those trying to get from Frankfort to Charlevoix—it's a potential traffic problem. For me, Traverse City is just home.

Throughout southern Michigan "Traverse City" is a name that conjures up images of big open water or lots of fresh snow. In contrast to the major-city throb of Detroit, Traverse City is a quiet small town. To about half a million people each year, Traverse City is the Cherry Festival.

In the phrase "I'm heading up to Traverse City," the locale "Traverse City" is used to mean a much larger region. Visitors heading north to Old Mission, Long Lake, the Boardman Valley, and even Interlochen describe their destination in the generic "Traverse City." When you tell someone from downstate that you are from Traverse City, they are likely to say, "Oh, I love the Sand Dunes." And they mean the Sleeping Bear Dunes, which lie a good 25 miles from the city limits. Traverse City is "Up North."

If you are from Manistee, Charlevoix, or Grayling, Traverse City is a trip to town. More than 100 years ago when the first European settlers farming along Lake Michigan needed supplies, they hitched up a wagon to head for Traverse City. As they have for more than a century our regional neighbors come to Traverse City for a day of shopping, dinner at a choice of restaurants, and

entertainment—once a show at the Opera House, now a movie in one of the multiplexes.

It was big local news when the Grand Traverse Mall opened, but in the ten years since, it has become only a small part of the shopping landscape that has defined the area south of the city limits. Despite your opinion of "Big Box" stores, if you want to stock up the pantry, find a new suit, fix up your house, and buy that new big screen TV all in one day, you are heading for the corner of US-31 and South Airport Road. Regionally, women shopping for a wedding or prom dress or men looking for power tools plan a day here. Retailing in Traverse City is admittedly a question of scale—Novi's Twelve Oaks Mall hosts more people on a busy December Saturday than live in all of Grand Traverse County—but regionally, Traverse City is a shoppers' Mecca.

Traverse City is my hometown. My family shops at the mall. We fly out of Cherry Capital Airport. We've even been known to eat an elephant ear or two at the Cherry Festival. But for us, Traverse City is something more. It's a place where we can live, work, and go to school while enjoying all of the things that most people only associate with vacations. We ride our bikes to the beach and watch the Blue Angels fly over our house. My wife cross-country skis from our front door and across the campus of Northwestern Michigan College. Both our children could downhill ski before they could ride a bike.

The photographs in this book are collected from my life. Some of these images were captured when I pulled off the road on my way to a meeting or on the way home from Wal-Mart. Others I found on my daily walks with my dog. There are days when I have forced myself to re-see the bay that has become as ordinary to me as the house across the street. On those journeys I am continually surprised at the art I find in the landscape just by looking for it. In every case these are common images, the things anyone can find among the increasing hustle of Traverse City. There are no secret locations. I had no special access.

In the end, the magic of Traverse City can be found in its everyday beauty. In a place where people can enjoy a comfortable life in a welcoming community, they can also find the quiet splendor of a walk in the woods or the breathtaking coda of a Great Lakes sunset—without even getting in a car. A million dollar cottage is not required; everyone is welcome. Traverse City is our hometown.

OPPOSITE PAGE: The Boardman River

OPPOSITE PAGE: Old Mission Point Light. The grounds are open to the public, but the light is a private residence.

The beach at Bayshore Resort, West Grand Traverse Bay

PREVIOUS PAGE SPREAD: East Grand Traverse Bay at Four Mile Road

The Martinek's Clock. Traverse City has left standard bicycles
throughout downtown for anyone who wants to use them.

A River Runs Through It

The Boardman River is undersold. It's not that the people of Traverse City don't cherish the resource, but that its many facets are so widely spread that they are difficult to see in one look. Starting in a swamp near Kalkaska, the Boardman turns into something we would call "a river" about 40 miles east of where it fills West Grand Traverse Bay. Along the way the Boardman gains volume from 18 creeks and 12 lakes throughout the region.

At its headwaters, the Boardman flows through lightly populated forestland, much of it publicly held. In these areas the river offers some of its most rustic recreational opportunities. Campers seeking pack-in isolation will find it easily in the Sand Lakes Quiet Area. The wetlands throughout the various creeks are home to countless birds and small animals as well as deer, bear, and coyote.

Once these creeks and other feeders develop into something that can be canoed or waded, the recreation opportunities change. The upper Boardman is home to both brown and brook trout, with many of its small tributaries functioning as nurseries for the wild trout. Fishing pressure is low, and at places like the Brown Bridge Quiet Area the wading is easy for even beginning fly-fishers. Recent and ongoing riverbank rehabilitation continues to improve the resource.

Where trout are happy, so will be humans looking for a place to navigate. Most of the Boardman system is open and accessible to canoes and kayaks. Compared to its peers—the Manistee, the AuSable, and the Betsie—canoe pressure is light and on all but the busiest weekends, floaters can enjoy a quiet paddle. The hushed murmur of the upper Boardman's flow seems particularly gentle in contrast to the almost urban feel of Traverse City so nearby. The proximity of "town" just a short drive away takes the edge off certain potentially risky endeavors. For example, the Boardman is an excellent place to try an early February canoe trip. Access roads are quickly cleared of even the heaviest snows and the bone-chilling cold seems less so when there is a tavern, fireplace, or warm bed nearby. Novice kayakers will find Brown Bridge Pond a welcoming first paddle.

Brown Bridge Pond is one of three dam ponds along the Boardman. The quiet pond is home to countless birds, including great blue heron, eagles, and every summer a pair of nesting loons. No wake is strictly enforced on the 200 acre pond, making it ideal for birding, paddle sports, and fishing. Traverse City maintains 1,300 acres of hiking and snowshoe trails around the pond. When the fall leaves reach peak color, the view of Brown Bridge Pond from the platform along the hiking trail is arguably the best Grand Traverse County has to offer. Like most of the Boardman's watershed, the Brown Bridge area is easily accessible, free to use, and offers something every season of the year.

In contrast to the relative seclusion of the ponds, the Boardman swells into a lake just as it encounters the noise and traffic of South Airport Road. Boardman Lake is perhaps most notable for the way it controls the east-west traffic flow of the city. City residents will plan a route for daily errands by mapping out a path around the lake.

The Traverse Area District Library overlooks the lake, and city offices lie along its northern banks. The two city post offices can be best described as "at opposite sides of Boardman Lake." Although it's ever-present in the center of town, Boardman Lake is also lightly used.

In the summer sun, Boardman Lake is upstaged by Grand Traverse Bay just a few blocks away. But an occasional fishing boat will dot its surface. Boardman Lake is home to pike, walleye, bluegill, and, every now and then,

a bass. Its greatest fishing pressure, however, is in the winter when anglers catch yellow perch through the ice. Once the ice is solid, a few shanties will appear and several fisherman can be seen with their white five-gallon bucket chairs and short tip-up rods.

In winter, hundreds of waterfowl gather at the south end of Boardman Lake where the constant flow of the river coming into the lake keeps the ice from freezing. When temperatures drop below zero, there is nowhere better to be than inside Auntie Pastas sipping a warm drink watching the ducks and swans paddling in the patches of open water, using the 35° river to keep warm.

Boardman Lake turns back into a river when it crosses 8th Street in the last few blocks of its journey to West Bay. The river adds immeasurable charm to Traverse City as it winds through downtown. Children and their fathers fish in the small pool just below the 8th Street falls. Couples stroll along the wooden boardwalk that follows the northern bank of the river as it flows under Union Street the first time. The Boardman glides west through a few neighborhood backyards until it turns back east and follows Front Street behind the businesses that turn their backs to the bay. When the river crosses back under Union Street for a second time, it becomes the background for the Farmers' Market, where kids run along its banks throwing bread to the ducks and watching the dark shadows of huge salmon heading upstream.

Humbly and without ceremony, the river makes its final turn north poised to provide nearly a third of the bay's water volume. After traveling more than 40 miles through swamps, forests, and backyards, unnoticed by the tourists on the Clinch Park beach or bike riders on the T.A.R.T. trail, the Boardman River disappears into Grand Traverse Bay in a graceful dénouement.

OPPOSITE AND ABOVE: Boardman Lake

Moomers Homemade Ice Cream, North Long Lake Road. From the deck outside, patrons can watch the cows that provide the cream from which Moomers' more than 50 flavors are made. No trip to Traverse City is complete without a taste of Michigan's best from this family farm.

Traverse City's Farmers' Market, between Cass and Union Streets north of Front Street.
The open-air market is open seasonally on Wednesday and Saturday mornings

The Reffitt Trail

Take a Walk

Dogs enjoy special status in Traverse City. Shops and offices all over town have workplace dogs. These are not drug-sniffing or seeing-eye dogs, but friendly greeters that meet you at the door with wagging tails. From the computer repair shop to the audiologist, Traverse Citians bring their dogs to work. Where there are people with dogs, there are people who need to take walks.

While the passion for dogs alone may not explain why, Traverse City is a walkers' paradise. Certainly the Victorian homes lining the sidewalks in Central Neighborhood invite an after-dinner stroll, and the one-mile loop at the Civic Center is perfect for a 30-minute jog. But Traverse City offers something more. Within a mile of anywhere in the city there is a quiet walk in the woods waiting.

Probably the least used of the hiking opportunities is Hickory Hills, just a few blocks up-hill to the west end of Randolph Street. Hickory Hills is best known as a 125-acre city-owned ski area where Traverse City teens learn to ski. Thanks to the foresight of visionary city leaders in the 1950s, this prime land is still open exclusively for recreation.

In summer the rolling Hickory Hills comprise one of Michigan's more difficult disc golf courses. To anyone with feet, Hickory Hills is a great hike waiting to be taken. In the warmer months hikers may encounter a frisbee foursome here and there, and the parking gets pretty tight after school in January and February; but over all, Hickory Hills is surprisingly quiet for an area less than a mile from the center of town. In the spring trillium and bellwort blanket the ground in white and yellow. When the trees are bare in winter the hilltops offer spectacular views of town.

Just ten blocks south of Hickory Hills, the Traverse City State Hospital grounds is a walkers dream. Still within the city limits, the acres of wooded trails and open meadows are isolated from traffic noise. My dog Bissell knows these trails well; we have hiked the grounds of the former Traverse City Asylum in all seasons, and the magic never fades. When the trails are covered in snow, Nordic skiers and snowshoers will find just enough variation in terrain to keep even the shortest trek interesting. Spring flowers are the first signs that winter is finally over. Summer bursts of pink rose hips throughout the trail system mark the places where the bright red berries on the bare trees will mark the same paths in winter. Throughout the grounds there are hidden treats. Creeks roam through the hills. Various abandoned structures invite the imagination to wander and several geocaches tempt children to come along.

A final hidden path in Traverse City wanders along the south side of the railroad tracks that lie behind the Traverse City State Park. With one trailhead at Parsons Road just east of Three Mile and second trail access hidden in a neighborhood off Four Mile, there is nothing remote about the Reffitt Trail. It's a straight line in-and-out trail, and in the summer you can hear the traffic roaring through town on US-31. Still, there is something charming about the Reffitt Trail. The Reffitt family preserved the valuable land just to keep it wooded. Development flanking the preserve on all sides tells the story of what would have become without the family's generosity. The Reffitt Trial says something about the people of Traverse City. We honor and value the place where we live, and we love our dogs.

Grounds of the former Traverse City Asylum

Have Some Pie

Traverse City's odd relative, if we have one, is the National Cherry Festival. People who live here have a love-hate relationship with the annual eight-day party. For one week of the year our hometown becomes a different place. Unknown authorities stretch ugly orange fencing along the most beautiful mile of highway in Michigan. Our precious Open Space is filled with giant inflatable marketing symbols. Half a million people come to crowd our streets and beaches. Yick. But then again, half a million people come to rent hotel rooms, eat meals, and buy things. We love the Cherry Festival.

What's not to love. Sure there are a very few cynics who make a show of scheduling vacations out of town during Cherry Festival, but the rest of us settle in for a weeklong smorgasbord of distraction. If nothing else, there's kids' pie-eating. In her first pie-eating contest my daughter, Madeline, watched other kids smashing their faces into their dishes but never took a bite. She was three. Over the years she has gone from awed spectator to contender, last year grabbing a win from a boy twice her size. While she has the advantage of a late July birthday—sometimes making her the oldest in her age group—strategy has been the key to her success.

Early on she learned it's not enough to finish first. You have to wave, jump up and down, and do anything you can to get the overwhelmed judges to notice you. It was a lesson learned with tears the year she finished eating first, and shyly sat while the judges raised the hands of others who were still chewing long after her plate was empty.

As she's matured, so has the competition. Simple tactics aren't enough now. She has developed the wear-the pie technique. It essentially involves rolling her face all over the plate to get the pie to stick to her head. "It's not what goes in your stomach, Dad," she tells me.

Madeline sizing-up the competition.

"It's how much isn't left on the plate." I'm so proud.

The excitement starts to build each year when the Blue Angels blast sonic booms over our house. The annual air show is scheduled for first Saturday and Sunday of the festival, but the roar of F/A-18s rattles windows all over town starting the Wednesday before Cherry Festival. The Blue Angels come only every other year; when they are in town each air-show can draw as many as 75,000 visitors, a crowd that puts US-31 into gridlock that would make New Yorkers jealous. The connection to cherries is unknown.

The cherry link is easier to find in the Cherry Festival's other headliner—the parades. Traverse City loves a parade, and during the eight-day festival there can be as many as four. Three parades, the Heritage, Junior Royale (with an "e"), and Cherry Royale ("e" again) are part of the regular schedule, and when the calendar doesn't put one of those on or near the Fourth of July, local patriots will make sure that Uncle Sam's birthday doesn't go unnoticed. Such parade density makes original content hard to come by, and many floats find their way on more than one trip down Front Street. Among the many parade choices, the one event that captures the essence of the cherry theme is the Heritage Parade.

The Heritage Parade is the ying to the Blue Angels yang. Although the festival's connection to cherries is sometimes

hard to find, it rides up front in the Heritage Parade. The four-block-long display of antique Farm-All and John Deere tractors is more than just a nod to a day gone-by; some come from the orchard to the parade in the same day. It's the first look the whole community gets of the Cherry Queen candidates as they ride atop a series of loaner convertibles. This funky blast from the past includes everything from baby-kissing politicians to high school baton twirlers, the VFW, UAW, and BSA.

And of course there are fireworks. Each year the festival closes with fireworks blasting over West Grand Traverse Bay on the evening of the eighth day. It always seems to come too soon. Eight days should be time enough to load

up on fun (and Gibby's Good Fries), but it never is. The schedule of events runs more than a page each day, and even Superman couldn't do it all in one year.

Madeline turns 12 this summer, so it's her last year to be seen in public smeared with pie. There used to be cherry pie eating for everyone, but like so many things related to actual cherries, that's gone. After this summer we'll have to get our festival thrills from all our other favorites. There's always the Blue Angels and the Heritage Parade—where else can you see a butcher from Cedar cranking meat and cherries into sausage in real-time on a float sporting a live polka band?

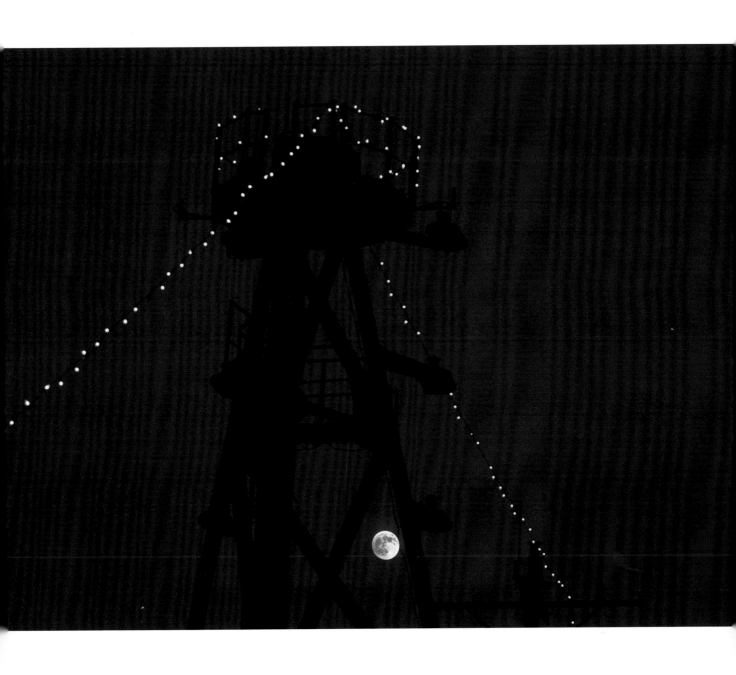

T.S. State of Michigan, Used for training at the Great Lakes Maritime Academy

SunnyBank.
This extraordinary private garden on Sixth Street is open to the
public when the small sign "Garden Open Today" is on the steps.

The Clock Tower, Northwestern Michigan College. Even with recent construction and growth, the NMC campus retains the fading tradition of carefully landscaped public outdoor spaces. Sculptures, plantings, walkways, and site lines throughout the campus are designed to offer something for the eye in every season.

Power Island.
Henry Ford once owned the island as
a hunting preserve, but sold it when
his stocked deer escaped across the ice
to the Old Mission Peninsula. This
public island west of Bower's Harbor
has rustic campsites and many hiking
trails. It is only accessible by boat.

The Great Lakes Maritime Academy at Northwestern Michigan College is one of six federally chartered Maritime Schools, and the only one on fresh water. Men and women from throughout the United States come to Traverse City to begin their seafaring careers.

OPPOSITE PAGE: West and East Grand Traverse Bays, View from Wayne Hill

Grounds of the former Traverse City Asylum